The Workplace Zoo

The
Workplace
Zoo

Karin Stangl

The Workplace Zoo

Contact Karin Stangl:
mariposa_verde@q.com

Mercury HeartLink
www.heartlink.com

Disclaimer

The Workplace Zoo is a collection of poems about relatable, fictitious characters that everyone has known in the workplace.

Most are composite characters, who everyone has encountered in a typical work environment.

None of these characters describe real people. Any descriptions that seem to be about real people are purely unintentional and coincidental. The author claims no liability for describing perceived real people living or dead.

The Workplace Zoo

*for my
Mother
Marie Stangl*

The Adder

Voracious, stealthy
Fork-tongued adder
Slithers up
The corporate ladder.

Takes down names
And loves to flatter.
Thrives upon
The back door chatter.

Fangs exposed,
Old victims scatter.
Ethics and people
Never matter.

Instinctive predator
Could not be gladder
Than to serve your head
On a silver platter.

Friends betrayed and wary.
Nothing's sadder
Than the loner's path
Of the corporate adder.

The Angelfish

Angel is special
Among the fishes.
She bats her eyes,
And gets her wishes.

She casts a spell
On a mid-life male.
By swishing her
Tantalizing tail.

Her cooing voice
And fresh flirtations
Belie her cunning
Manipulations.

No ethics or conscience.
Morals run askew.
Her female friends
Are but a few.

Her last boss' wife
Was soon his ex.
He was tempted by angel's
Aptitude for sex.

She dangles enticement
Most persistent.
Until elevated from secretary
To special assistant.

This fish's pheromones
Pander danger.
Beware this fetching
Naughty angel.

The Barracuda

Old barracuda's
Swift and powerful jaws
Embrace the exactness
Of corporate laws.

Analytical mind
Abhors stupidity.
No emotions or mercy.
Imposes strict rigidity.

Preys on colleagues.
Preys on naiveté.
Gulping down the weak gets them
Out of the way.

He has no tact.
Exhibits no class.
Never misses opportunities
To chew someone's ass.

Considers all explanations
As lame excuses.
Expects employees to steal
And commit abuses.

Touts his great intellect
Expects perfection.
Hyper-critical of flaws.
Advocate of pop inspections.

Lives alone, sharpens his teeth.
To his reputation he's blind.
This carnivorous dictator
Attacks and eats his own kind.

The Chameleon

An elusive lizard
Who, whenever he's near,
Says exactly what he thinks
You want to hear.

Next person he meets
His story has changed.
Priorities
Now rearranged.

Hard to pin down.
Message answers his phone.
His excuses change
With his mood and tone.

You try to grab hold.
He slithers off without fail.
You're left holding
A detached reptilian tail.

He promptly grows a new one
To cover his end.
Chameleon is everybody's
New best friend.

Tongue is evasive.
You haven't a clue,
That he's committed to tasks
To be dumped on you.

He'll tell you he's done it.
But it really sat on the shelf.
Don't depend on the chameleon
Just do it yourself.

The Ferret

The ferret is
Nobody's friend.
He is the deputy boss
Why should he pretend?

A law degree gives him
Superior intellect.
You do not impress.
Likes to inspect.

A millennial,
With key essentials.
Promoted by political friends,
Without credentials.

Experience lacking,
Relies on bloated connections
He'll be a fair-weather ally
Without exceptions.

You've just been run over
By a Mack truck diesel.
You're just a stepping stone.
For this little weasel.

The ferret's soft fur
Makes him seem a pet.
But, he's the most arrogant jerk
You've ever met.

The Fly

Musca Domestica,
Propelled phantom pest.
Flits through everyone's privacy.
Social insect to avoid and detest.

Transports, like bacteria,
Gossip, ill will, scandal, and lies.
Views all innuendo and rumor
Through compounded eyes.

The fly has no reverence.
Open sores whet insatiable taste.
Immersed in filth, dung, and garbage.
Spawns in fermented waste.

Whirring incessant annoyance
Performs elusive aerial gyrations.
Who has sticky proboscis licked
To get more information?

No-pest-strip barricades posted.
Buzzes past them with ease.
Lives vicariously through others.
Gossip spreads like contagious disease.

Nimble nuisance ignores swats and swipes.
Displays relentless persistence.
Oh for a well-aimed Flit-gun
To end your pesky existence.

The Gecko

Computer screens mirror
Gecko's face, week after week.
Gecko's a focused
Computer geek.

Speaks languages understood only
By other techs.
Wears tennis shoes
And wire specs.

Down time dabbles
On computer games.
Desk pictures of pets
With weird Star Trek names.

Geckos are tenacious.
Most are unobtrusive.
About their private lives
They are most elusive.

Geckos are proud
To be computer techs.
Fringes of Generation "Y"
And Generation "X."

Geckos slither in, do their jobs,
Then slither out.
An odd breed of lizard
Without a doubt.

The Goat

Skips his showers.
No olfactory sense.
The goat practices
Hygienic negligence.

Cigar smoke
In his shirt still lingers.
Onion rings and yesterday's lunch
Are on his fingers.

Yellow-green teeth produce
Noxious breath to share.
A strong garlic aroma
Taints the air.

Coffee stains his tie.
Clothes are full of wrinkles.
Forgets to wash his hands
After he tinkles.

Eats something that in his teeth
A toothpick speared.
Buffet still clinging
To his beard.

Fast food sacks and cartons
Top his clutter piles.
Hasn't seen his desktop
In quite a while.

The rumpled goat
Has flaws extensive.
Cannot help
But be offensive.

The Jackal

Keen eyes observe.
His jowls he licks.
Jackal watches on sly
Office politics.

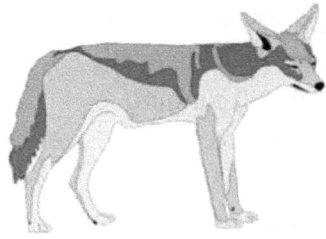

Eager ears pricked.
Poised to fetch with zeal
Promotions or scraps
He may chance to steal.

Performs menial scutwork
With greyhound strides.
Watches other dogs on the job
With rabid anger inside.

Seething contempt for those
Who yelp and bay.
He growls, snarls, and whines.
Then slinks away.

Attention fixed on the jugular by day.
He sleeps hungry at night.
When prey is feeble and dying
Joins pack to maul them on sight.

Distempered relations with others.
They kick with biting remarks.
Clever jackal mimics Basenji.
Revenge waits, never barks.

The Kite

With stolen company pens
She makes quick changes.
The credit bylines
She rearranges.

Hardly noticed.
She's barely seen
Making personal copies
At the Xerox machine.

The copying kite
Only hesitates
To eavesdrop and listen.
And, then...she waits.

A cautious eye
Keeps sharply abreast
For snatches from snitches
To feather her nest.

Was it your idea?
Well, it was <u>hers</u>, too.
With ease she makes
A fool of you.

When she's hungry
This sly, soaring wanna be
Does whatever it takes
To ride for free.

She collects your kudos
Then, skirts away.
She swallows whole
Unsuspecting prey.

The Lamb

Airy-headed little lamb.
Hair's blond as platinum snow.
Anything of key importance
She most surely will not know.

Was it Mr. Knight who called?
Or, was it Mr. Day?
"It's on a scrap of paper," bleats the lamb,
"I must have thrown away."

She loses the originals.
Mind seems in outer space.
Typing simple forms and letters
Require Wite Out by the case.

Takes hours making copies.
Yet staples pages out of order.
Makes frequent trips to restrooms
Or visits friends just down the corridor.

Memos with typos never spell-checked.
Never focused. Never there.
The day is one big frequent break.
Always vacant is her chair.

Prompt at 5:00 o'clock she's ready
Out the front door she'll merrily blow.
Those she fleeced now call her "mutton-head"
And vow: "This lamb has got to go!"

The Leech

Embodies integrity and brilliance
Of an annelid worm.
Attained mid-level management on talents
To adapt, pucker, wriggle, and squirm.

Pliable segmented abilities.
Filled with anemic creative juices.
Sucks others' hard work and hemoglobin.
Is quick to render excuses.

Comes in late, then leaves early.
Out of town for the day.
Leech takes work-related vacations.
Lets the company pay.

Loves to delegate work.
A carnivorous, insincere sort.
Sticking unwarranted two-cents in
Is her favorite sport.

Insecure plagiarist says
Those she's drained dry are friends.
At social gatherings clings to the wall
For appearances, hangs on 'til the end.

Questionable awards and diplomas
Adhere to walls in every direction.
Resumé's watery references to notables
Alleged are connections.

Parasite's supplied in reserve
With gumption and gall.
Rooted like a barnacle adhesive
Will likely outlast us all.

The Magpie

Sees only black or white.
No shades of grey.
Focuses for a moment,
Then, flits away.

Desk is cluttered
With languishing piles.
Office walls display artwork
In eclectic styles.

Dangle a new, shiny project
Alert magpie is poised to snatch.
Months later it sits in the
Yet-to-do batch.

Magpie bites life like grapes
To savor in bunches.
Adept at skiing, golf,
And, of course, power lunches.

Magpie always struggles.
Runs short and runs late.
Forgets people's names
And confuses key dates.

Cell phone calls are
A constant interruption.
Distracted magpie is not
Lacking of gall or of gumption.

Blows in late for meetings.
Then, to capture attention
Interjects off-the-wall opinions
That create group dissension.

Sees only black or white
No shades of grey.
Magpie drops the ball
Then, flies away.

The Mice

Mice have furry tails,
Big ears and stubble.
They scurry by.
They don't cause trouble.

Mice have stealthy,
Meek, or silent voices.
They are never asked
To express their choices.

They don't have opinions.
They just agree.
When conflict arises,
They're the first to flee.

Silent and diligent.
Most think they're nice.
They do their work.
They pay the price.

Behind closed doors
Mice often cling,
But, observant eyes
See everything.

They don't climb the ladder.
They don't aspire.
They skirt the floorboards
Until they retire.

The Ostrich

With long, powerful legs
Running away, she's speedy.
A gangling goose of a boss
Who's scared and needy.

Voicing concerns or problems
Could result in a peck.
Because an ostrich will <u>never</u>
Stick out her neck.

Indecision and fear
Define her as a leader.
She likes free-range praise,
So don't forget to feed her.

She'll back you up, if safe
To make a stand,
But prefers to bury her head
In comfortable sand.

When all arrows have landed
Her head, it emerges.
She often acts flighty
On the most primal of urges.

To get what she wants
She fawns and begs.
At times she's been know to lay
Huge verbal eggs.

The ostrich is clueless,
With insecurities stricken.
Some say her backbone
Is akin to the chicken.

The Oyster

Uncontroversial, anti-clamorous.
The oyster's calm in the storm.
The oyster's productive.
The oyster's the norm.

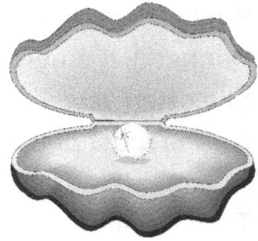

Endures with patient indifference.
Outer shell's a calcified shield.
Favors gentle purling of waters.
Knows when to yield.

Taciturn, benign disposition.
Ebbs in and out with the tide.
A tenacious survivor.
Keeps feelings inside.

During reorganizations and layoffs,
Hinges seal airtight, half against half.
Endures chafing criticism from others.
Applies inner calcareous salve.

The oyster's mostly a loner,
In contentious water he swirls.
Surmounts the pressure and conflict.
Spits forth work-product pearls.

The Pack Rat

Pencils, clips, CDs,
And pens galore
Are squirreled away in
The pack rat's drawer.

The watchful gatekeeper
Hordes supplies.
No one gets past
Her beady eyes.

Items are hidden in stashes
Around her room,
In case a budget cut
Should chance to loom.

Supply catalogs
Are stacked in piles.
She advocates reusing
Old manila files.

Just one writing implement
Requires her permission.
Requests result in questions
And suspicion.

She is a thrifty rodent.
She is resourceful.
She tells you, "no," and
Is not remorseful.

There is no doubt
Frugal pack rat saves.
Workers who need supplies
Must become her slaves.

The Parrot

She's a painted crow.
Everyone agrees.
Enjoying gilded cage
And amenities.

Binocular eyes
Keep a vigil search
For proximal movements
That threaten her perch.

Quick-to-ruffle feathers
Are preened neatly in place.
The boss' snitch struts
With the loftiest grace.

Wearing designer shoes,
Matching suits and vests,
Her vivid plumage roosts
In tar-feathered nests.

Ever guarding parameters
Of her caged domain
Mocks with contempt other fowl
Who are simple or plain.

Masticates seeds to a pulp
With her tough, old beak.
Symbol of pecking order
That devours the weak.

One day she graces you
With the time of day.
The next, you're snatched by talons
Of a bird of prey.

Skills and vocabulary limited.
Voice cackles shrill and clear—
Pretty bird repeats what
Higher-ups want to hear.

The Raccoon

He whistles a happy
Carefree tune.
A clever bandit
Black-and-white raccoon.

From off your desk
He borrows ball point pens.
Never returns ones he took
But, comes back again.

Takes the last cup of coffee
And makes no more.
Leaves trails of trash and debris
On his office floor.

Leaves the Xerox lid up
And completely out of paper.
He always has a hand
In the latest caper.

He'll eat your lunch
Out of the refrigerator.
He's a sneaky backroom
Instigator.

Responsible for creating
Colossal project messes.
Then, stealthily
He acquiesces.

Asks for help in doing
Mundane reports.
While you do his work
He quick departs.

He'll take your notes.
He'll steal your chair.
You'll notice phantom paw prints
Everywhere.

The Raven

Poe's messenger likens
Chicken Little in black.
"The world's self-destructing!"
"The world's under attack!"

Melancholic moods conjured
For those starved and who've bled.
No power to change things.
Martyrs causes instead.

The sensitive raven
Cries tears with the rain.
"Why is half the world warring?"
"The other half suffering pain?"

"The day you're born you start dying,"
Wails the raven with rage.
So, he goes into mourning,
And hides for days in his cage.

"Ethiopia! Another plane crash!"
"Economic depression!"
Spreads pessimism like plague
With morbid, neurotic obsession.

Morning coffee's laced with Valium,
To savor daily news discourses.
Fondness for gory headlines, obituaries,
Bad weather, divorces.

Raven's catastrophic concerns,
Addressed with screeches and bellows,
Dropping mundane tasks, work-related
Into the arms of his fellows.

The Rhino

She's selfish,
Opinionated, surly, rude.
The rhino's got
An attitude.

Rhino storms in,
She paws and snorts.
(Who'd dare say she's too overweight
For those mini shorts.)

She's tenacious and testy
Until she gets her way.
Say "no." She takes her marbles
And will refuse to play.

She sticks in
Her protruding, obnoxious horn.
So, most places she's been
Her welcome's worn.

Tell her your problems,
She knows how to fix it.
An idea, not hers,
She's quick to nix it.

A divorcee, a regular
At clubs and singles' bars.
Her tough old skin
Bears battle scars.

If you become an obstacle
In her path,
And vex her plans
You'll feel her wrath.

The Rooster

Red-faced rooster
Full of stories
About the good old days
And faded glories.

Loves to boast
And draw a crowd.
Opinions on the reorg
Shrill and loud.

He preens. He struts.
He picks each nit.
Will never change his mind
Or adapt, one bit.

Fears new ideas,
New foreign ways.
Hangs on to same old.
Plots sabotage, delays.

Living in the box
Brings satisfaction.
Likes the way things are.
Creates distraction.

Stirs up and scares
The weak and feeble.
Paradigm shifts are deemed
Dangerous and evil.

He drags his feet.
Mounts grapevine defense.
Young pullets listen
At the picket fence.

Silly rooster
Is the first to crow.
Stubborn pride leads him to being
The first let go.

The Seal

Brings in doughnuts
Almost every morn.
Loves to toss out balls
And toot his horn.

Social seal thrives
On constant attentions.
Embraces texting, the norm.
Loves to attend conventions.

Seal barks out loud.
He cracks his knuckles.
Loves diversion, amusement.
Snorts when he chuckles.

Tells stupid jokes.
Hums silly ditties.
A ready volunteer
Loves work on committees.

Seal is motivated most
By kudos and praise.
Boss keeps a pail of fish handy
To reward good days.

Spouts his personal views.
Knows how everyone feels.
Loves to swim in formation
With up-and-coming seals.

Cell phone is frequently
Stuck to an ear like glue.
Champions causes
Without a clue.

Seals like to swim in the loop.
Rumor purveyors.
Throw some fish, keep in-the-know,
And they're great team players.

The Skunk

The skunk emits
The most obnoxious fumes.
Her scent precedes her
As she enters rooms.

Red nails remove the atomizer
From her purse.
She spritzes more cheap perfume
And the scent grows worse.

Eyes roll back. Throats burn.
Co-workers gasp for air.
She's even perfumed
Her poofed up hair.

Customers wince.
Her neighbors pale.
No one dares to
Chance inhale.

She's oblivious to others'
Olfactory sense overload
One whiff and nasal passages
Just corrode.

The skunk's fragrant fumes
Can't be underestimated.
Head outdoors,
Or be asphyxiated.

The Swordfish

Silver-haired swordfish
Swims in tropical seas.
Slices through distortion.
Does not aim to please.

No tolerance for stupidity
Or corporate maneuvers.
Disdain for the up-and-coming
Shakers and movers.

Watches nippers
From prestigious schools
Swim right past him
Into executive pools.

Preys on small fish
Who tend to stray.
Swallows those
Who disobey.

Demoted director of the old guard
But as a manager stayed.
This savvy survivor knows
How the game is played.

Eats lunch alone each day
At the corner deli.
Hides his vulnerable,
Soft underbelly.

Works best in isolation.
Never complains or whines.
On retirement track
Just marking time.

The Toad

Yellow slit-eyes are wary.
His attention span's brief.
Massive weight unsupported
By the company chief.

Wearing full-cut tailored suits
To disguise noticeable flab.
Takes pond scum to lunch
On the company tab.

Rewards those who toady.
Calls his toadstool the throne.
Laurels tinged slimy green
Like money skimmed as his own.

Leapfrog scars camouflaged.
Belches tales of success.
Ceaseless complaints of an ulcer.
Yet, he drinks to excess.

Overgrown polliwog devours
Unsuspecting bug with a snap.
Croaks a few orders.
And then, takes a nap.

The Tom Cat

He saunters to work.
Everybody's pal.
The tom cat's always
On the prowl.

In the secretarial pool
He likes to linger.
Wedding band fits loosely
On his finger.

New female workers
Are like catnip.
Eyes focus on breasts,
And leg, and lip.

He oozes charm.
His purr finesses.
He likes to give back rubs
And soft caresses.

He's oh so helpful to
The attractive and new.
Just a wealth of experience
He can share with you.

"That dress looks great!"
"Are you getting thinner?"
Flattery ends
With invites out to dinner.

Despite a file full
Of sexual harassment claims,
He continues to play
His courtship games.

If one dares get involved
Know he's still within reach...
Of a wife who has him
On an extended leash.

About the Author

Karin Stangl is a poet from Albuquerque, New Mexico. She is a member of New Mexico Poetry Alliance, New Mexico Poetry Society, and Fresh Ink writing groups.

Her award-winning poetry has been published in *Muse with Blue Apples, Cranberry Beads, Willow Street Magazine, Turtle Music Anthology, Crosswinds Magazine, The Southwest Poet, Compass Points*, and *Along the Rio Grande: Poetry from New Mexico*, among other publications. She has bachelor's and master's degrees from the University of New Mexico. She is currently a public relations consultant in Albuquerque.